I0426692

ORIGIN

OF THE

CONTINENTS

An Introduction to the Theory of

THE LITHOLOGIC CYCLE

By

Max B. Frederick

Printed in the United States of America

FIRST EDITION 1996
REPRINTED MARCH, 2003
REPRINTED AUGUST, 2003
REPRINTED SEPTEMBER, 2003
REPRINTED APRIL, 2004
SECOND EDITION OCTOBER, 2006
THIRD EDITION JULY, 2008
REPRINTED DECEMBER, 2014

ISBN: 978-1-312-79847-2

Readers are invited to correspond with the author at:

Max. B. Frederick, Publishing
146 Laurel St.
Central Point, OR 97502
Lithologic@earthscience.us

PREFACE

This is intended to be not only a scientific writing, but also an exercise in philosophy. The cold hard facts of science have a profound influence on our lives. Fact is fact, belief or denial does not change fact. However we all live by what we believe, not the mere acceptance of some idea, but the profound driving force that causes us to take the actions that we do. We all have belief systems that are part scientific and part religious. Some of our beliefs are based on scientific first hand knowledge of fact. Other beliefs are based on our religious confidence in the beliefs of someone we trust. What we believe affects the way we live our lives. What we believe has a profound influence on how we react to scientific fact. However, there is a clear and distinct line that cannot be crossed. What we believe now, or in the future, whether it be scientific, philosophic, or religious, does not change the true fact of what happened in the past. History revisionists have a profound influence on what we believe happened in the past, but revising history does not change what really happened. Scientific fact, principles and mechanisms in action in our environment do not depend upon our understanding nor our descriptions. These descriptions, whether you call them theories or beliefs, only help us to live within the bounds of the forces that exist. They do not change the facts to conform to our concepts.

Science does not prove religion or philosophy, nor does religion or philosophy prove science. True science and true religion, to be true, must both have no argument with true fact. As a logical extension, true science and true religion must have no argument with each other

We do not know the real truth of the past. We only have evidence. That evidence has been interpreted in various different ways depending on the philosophy of the interpreter. Since we do not really know what really happened how do we arrive at a best guess? We gather what may be our best guesses together and compare them with the evidence. In the process, we sometimes come up with new ideas. Sometimes, in the process, we recognize new evidence.

Currently there are two competing philosophies presenting evidence and guesses on the past history of the world. Without rigorous definition, they are the philosophies of science, and the authorities of religion. One might also include in religion the legends of the past from various cultures. I do not want to get caught up in the controversy. I only want to sort out the truth. The best I can hope for is to sort out the known truth from the guesses. I may also hope for putting some relative credibility estimate on some of those that remain guesses. Science has a notorious record of changing it's mind on what it believes to be the truth or on what it will recognize a evidence. Religion has a notorious record of disagreement from one religion to another and from one interpreter of their primary authority to another. Neither are credible as an authority on scientific fact. Science is only a tool to work with the known, not an authority on the unknown. Religion's only valid claim is to be an authority on philosophic and historic matters, not on scientific explanations. However, both science and the historic records of religion have much to offer.

As an example of the roles of Science and Religion, lets take the question of the maximum flood level that has occurred in the past and we can expect to see in the future.

Current science has recognized mechanisms that can cause floods, but not to the magnitude that are described in the eye witness accounts claimed by religion. Without a mechanism that can be used to explain the flood described in the claimed eye witness account, scientists tend not to accept the account as being anything more than myth or legend exaggerated far out of proportion. Religious scholars insist that the same account claims to be an actual eye witness account. Without acceptance of the account being what it claims to be, their religion cannot be accepted to be what it claims to be. Here is where science is used by anti-religion philosophers to over step the bounds of science. They claim that in the absence of science recognizing any mechanism which would cause a flood of such a magnitude, that there is not such a mechanism and such a flood did not happen, and therefore the religion is false. Furthermore, I have recognized the unwillingness of scientists. Convinced of the absence of such a mechanism they resist evidence indicating such a mechanism. In the same way, I have recognized the resistance of religious scholars to take another look at their authoritative writings to reassess their current interpretation of what their primary authority actually says. There is also the tendency for religious scholars to expect scientists to change their mind, thereby proving their religion is true. That is also a fallacy. Science changing it's mind and allowing that such a flood is within the realm of possibility, or even that such a flood actually happened cannot prove a religion to be true. It is only evidence that the account may have had it's origin in an eye witness account of a flood of such a magnitude.

By this logic, science cannot prove any religion to be true, or false. That is not the question. The question to be addressed in this writing is the scientific truth of a concept that may meet with resistance to be accepted solely because it may lend scientific credibility to events previously deemed incredible by scientific minds.

As I write this Preface on the Sixth day of January, 1997, I look back on this past week which many have described as the one Hundred Year Flood in the Central Valley of California. I am sitting high and dry three miles South of the Tuolumne River. This past week the Tuolumne river reached a height never before recorded by official records. However there are other records not recognized by our weather bureau. The land I am currently on is itself a record of the river being at a higher level. It is soil deposited by the river when it overflowed its banks in the unrecorded past. Hundreds of overflows in the unrecorded past have resulted in broad natural levies. It is on the slope of one of these natural levies that I am sitting right now.

The concept of a "hundred year flood" is commonly understood to be that flood which we must prepare for because we know it has happened in the past and will happen again, probably within about a hundred years. One philosophy is to enjoy the use of the land between floods and move out when the flood comes. Another is to engineer structures to prevent the flood from driving us from the land.

More subtle in the concept of the "hundred year flood" is that there is another step up in the magnitude of floods. We know from the evidence of the natural levies and the flood plains, from the experience of other countries where there are records going back thousands of years that the Thousand year flood is a valid concept. The unlimited extension of this concept is that there is an unimaginable level of flood in an unimaginable number of years. But that does not bother us because we cannot imagine that happening in our lifetimes nor in the foreseeable future. Besides that, the mechanism that causes the floods, the Hydrologic Cycle, has practical physical limits. There is not enough water around the earth to significantly raise sea level, and water is liquid and runs off into the sea.

With the development of the theory of the Lithologic Cycle comes the stark realization that the unimaginable flood of the unimaginable number of years is more likely fact than legend. We now have a mechanism that is actually operating that has the capability to raise sea level to the unimaginable height for the short duration of the unimaginable flood. With the acceptance of the existence of this mechanism comes the natural explanation and easy acceptance of the at least five mass extinctions of the geologic record. The many prior theoretical explanations of these mass extinctions all fall short in many areas that the unimaginable flood easily explains. This unimaginable flood now becomes imaginable as the physical limit of flood we can expect in the future.

The questions remain. Now that we can believe the threat of the unimaginable flood, what do we do with that belief? Now that we are beginning to understand the mechanism that causes that unimaginable flood, is there anything we can do to prevent or delay that flood? If there is, are we willing and motivated enough to do it?

Max B. Frederick

Ceres, California
January 6, 1997

TABLE OF CONTENTS

ABSTRACT AND CONCLUSION

The forces and mechanisms which have separated the lighter rocks of the continents from the heavier rocks of the ocean floor and have gathered those rocks together into continents seem obvious from what is now known and observed. The elements of erosion, subduction, and uplift combine into the Lithologic Cycle that includes a long quiet period of time like the one that we are currently living in where the mountains are eroding away, the continental area is spreading out, and the sea level is relatively constant. Also included in that cycle is an episode of mountain building. During a short period of time (several months at most) light (less dense) rock material is gathered and shoved down under the continents by runaway subduction. This adds to the roots of the mountains buoying them up in the rebound phase which follows the runaway subduction phase. This mountain building episode also includes a mass extinction and fossil deposition due to flooding of the ocean over the continents. Five major mass extinctions are recognized in the geologic record. At least two mass extinctions are mentioned in recorded history. There is no scientific reason why this could not happen again at any time.

PREVIEWS OF SOME DETAILS OF THE THEORY

This continental flooding is due to a multiple Kilometer rise in the level of the ocean floor as the old cold heavy (more dense) ocean floor sinks under the continent. This old cold ocean floor is replaced by lighter hot ocean floor in an episode of runaway subduction (rapid sinking of the ocean floor under the continent). This sinking of the old ocean floor is due to the instability of more dense cold ocean floor rock being over less dense hot rock. The rapidity of the turnover may be due to the same mechanism that is observed in earthquakes where imperceptible creep is suddenly replaced by multiple mile per hour movement as the strain and deformation rate builds up to the point of flash liquefaction of the rocks at the contact zone. This flash liquefaction reduces the viscosity of the rocks in this slipping contact zone similar to a sudden injection of lubricant. This sudden lubrication of the slipping contact enables a nine order of magnitude change of velocity of the relative movement. This may be exactly what happens in an earthquake as it leaves evidence of the flash liquefaction in the form of a thin sheet of "slickensides" where the rocks slid along the fault.

PRESENTATION PHILOSOPHY

This is not intended to be a rigorous proof presentation of a theory. It is rather, to be a philosophical presentation of a new concept in the form of a theory. It is not necessary to prove the truth. If the theory represents truth, then scientific observations will prove it out. If the theory is not the way things really are, then scientific observations will prove it wrong. It is not up to me to prove the truth, but rather to stimulate scientists in the pursuit of truth.

This presentation is intended to be understandable by the scientist and the general public alike. Too long have we scientists isolated our ideas from the general public by our unique language and presentation style. It is time for the general population to be included in stimulating thought about the physical world we live in. We need to stimulate our students to be interested in science. Rather than complain that we are becoming a nation of scientific illiterates, we need to interest our people in scientific ideas. We need to make our writings more stimulating to the general public.

The writing style of modern legal and scientific writings is precise and non-redundant using highly specialized specific language. Much of this language is known only within the circle of those in the particular profession for which the writing is intended. For each meaning, a precisely defined word is selected and then used consistently throughout any particular article. If the reader does not understand the term, the reader is lost from the beginning. If the same precise term is constantly reused it does not stimulate new ideas, but stifles the scientists creativity. The majority of scientists dare not be different.

They dare not be the source of new ideas to depart from the present day accepted standard.

Ancient writings used a different style of writing. They used a style of writing that would survive translation even when the meaning of a word was not specific. The context would bridge the lapse. The important concepts were conveyed in parallel redundancy. The same thing would be said in a different way using different words. If the meaning were unclear in one or the other of the statements, the other wording would clarify the meaning. If the meaning were ambiguous in both statements, the common meaning was that meaning to be communicated.

In my style of writing I prefer the latter to the former. I prefer to state important concepts in different wordings in multiple reiterations. This causes the reader to think rather than to memorize. A modern style writing can be read completely with complete recognition of each word, but with no understanding of what was intended to be communicated. My style of writing requires not just recognition, but understanding of the terms for the reader to realize that different terms are referring to the same concept in a different way. Without complete understanding of the basic concepts my writing can appear to be nonsense to a highly educated reader expecting the modern style.

I prefer my style of writing because it parallels my style of thinking. If a nonsense concept is stated precisely and formally, it can take on an air of respectability and many times sound plausible. If the idea is re-phrased in different ways, if the concept is couched in different terms, the concept can be clearly seen to be pure bunk. This style of thinking sorts out in my mind the relevant from the chaff.

This rephrasing in different words of the concept or idea in my mind can point out the fallacy of my logic. Using this technique I can sort out the relevant from the irrelevant. Once I clearly understand my own idea, I can be sure of it's validity and communicate precisely the same idea to others without precise language.

To illustrate, if I were to give you the assignment of restating the basic concepts in that previous paragraph without using any of the basic idea conveying words that I used, you might come up with the following to illustrate that you clearly understood what I was saying. "If I state it in enough assorted ways, anyone can comprehend my hypothesis, anyone of normal IQ can judge the validity of my thesis." With this clearly in mind, now you are ready to read my writings.

THE PROBLEM

Why are there continents? One would think that a question like that would have been already answered. This is a time of esoteric questions having to do with the likes of the warping of time and space. I have talked with many seventh and eighth grade science students and I get the idea that they believe all the simple questions have been answered. This is not true. In a way, we, as scientists, have not advanced far in our way of thinking from the times we criticize. We are critical of the times when people believed that the earth was flat, frogs came from mud and flies came from meat. To us the truth in these areas is obvious. Yet, we have been faced with the obvious in many other areas and have not recognized it.

Many years ago in the late 1960's or early 1970's when I was a geology student at San Jose State College, I had a hard time with an essay question that Dr. Steven Skapinsky ask on one of his exams. He wanted me to choose and defend my choice of which mechanism was responsible for the building of the continents: The choices were Continental accretion or Continental Drift. (The term "Plate Tectonics" was not yet popularized.) I did not think either of the then current theories was adequate alone and got marked down on my answer. This was quite traumatic to me as I had been a 4.0 student. Later I went to a talk by J. Tuzo Wilson, an early pioneer in the popularization of plate tectonics and talked to him personally. I was still bothered by the lack of satisfactory explanation of the mechanism for driving the plates.

Why is the lighter rock gathered into continents? Why is it not just another layer spread out covering the whole surface of the earth above the heavier rock, and covered itself by a uniform depth of ocean of about two miles or more? These are still good questions. While others are asking high minded questions about the far reaches of the universe, time, and space, I am still not satisfied with the answers we have about the things closer to home. What are those "mountain building episodes" that many geology textbooks refer to without explanation of a mechanism? What is the mechanism driving the mountain building episodes? What is it that piles rock upon rock until it stands over three miles above the average sea floor level and sticks up far above sea level. Is the mechanism that builds the mountains the same mechanism that builds and holds the continents together?

THE NON-EXISTENT STABLE EARTH

Without a mechanism operating to build continents the entire earth would be covered with water an average of two miles deep. Without a mechanism operating to gather the lighter rocks on the surface of the ocean floor into clumps that stand over three miles high to stick out of the ocean, there would be no continents on the earth. If the outer layers of the earth were uniformly separated into layers it would be like this: Of course the outer layer would be as it is, air. Under the air would be a layer of water, the ocean, approximately two and a half miles deep covering the entire earth. That water would have a specific gravity of about 1.0. Under the water would a layer of rocks with a general composition of silicon and aluminum and a specific gravity of 2.6 to 2.7. That is about 2.6 to 2.7 times as dense as the water above. These are the rocks that generally compose the continents. With these continental rocks spread all over the ocean floor it would be a layer approximately five miles thick. Five miles is about the thickness of the solidified rock that actually makes up the ocean floor. Under the spread out and solidified continental rocks would be the same stuff that is actually under the sea floor and the continents now. That stuff is the mantle. The mantle is made up of rocks in a somewhat liquid state. The mantle, at least near the surface, is composed of the rock material of magnesium and Iron. This material when molten, has a specific gravity of approximately 3.0, a little more dense than the solid rocks above. This mantle layer is several hundred miles thick. Below that mantle layer are other layers, each more dense than the one above.

This picture I have painted of the composition of the outer layers of the earth would be a highly stable situation where each layer was lighter than the layer below. Each layer would actually be floating on top of the layer below. There would not be any continents standing over three miles above the sea floor and sticking out of the water as islands. This is not like the real world.

(Insert here two drawings illustrating the hypothetical earth interior cross section view if there were no continent gathering cycle and the actual cross section

THE REAL WORLD NON-STABLE EARTH

The real world is not like that. The real world is unstable in multiple ways. The continental areas are stable as far as the layering being increasingly dense as the depth increases, but they have an unstable tendency to spread out because they are three mile high structures surrounded by water that is much less dense. And they are made of material that on the large scale of continents is so weak that it cannot hold itself up when not supported from underneath. But the continents cover only about a third of the surface of the mantle. Now here is the real instability. With the less dense rock material gathered into continents, that leaves the mantle material exposed to the cold ocean water over two thirds of the earth. This mantle material has cooled and solidified to a depth of approximately five miles. When the rock material of the mantle cools and solidifies, it shrinks. It becomes more dense. It's specific gravity becomes approximately 3.2. With a specific gravity of 3.2, it is more dense than the liquid below with a specific gravity of 3.0. Rock material that has a greater density than the molten material beneath has a tendency to sink into the molten material below.

So the questions remain. Why did the continents form? What prevents them from spreading out to become a stable layering of the earth surface?

Think about it. How strong are rocks on the large scale? Rocks sometimes stand straight up in high cliffs. Sometimes a cliff will overhang a little. If rock were very strong you would think you would see cliffs with a great overhang where it had been undermined by a stream or ocean waves. Can you conceive of a cliff with an overhang of five or ten miles? A mile? Even a few hundred feet? No. On the large scale, rocks are not very strong. On the scale of the continents compared to your back yard, rocks are no stronger than an uneven pile of sand. Suppose you had a scale model of a continent in your back yard. Sand would be a reasonable strength material from which to build it. You certainly would not want a material so strong that you could pick it up by one side and it not break into millions of pieces. No, sand would be a good choice. Pile your sand up the scale equivalent of three miles above the ocean floor and then surround it with water about two or three times as broad as your continent. If you have ever tried to build an island in a fish tank using sand you know that before long your continent would be spread out all over your back yard under the water unless you had something to occasionally scoop the sand back into your continent.

Geologists looking at the continents now realize that the continents are eroding away into the oceans faster than they are growing to make up for the loss by erosion. That is why they talk of mountain building episodes in the past. They talk of the ultimate end of the continents as being a "peneplain", a plain at or near sea level. I'll go further than that. Once the continents reach the peneplain stage, tidal waves and ocean currents would wash over the land reducing the continents to below sea level. That is if there were no mechanism to counteract the effects of erosion.

If the earth is a few billion years old then the continents should have been spread out over the bottom of the oceans millions of years ago. As a matter of fact there should have never been any continents unless there is a very powerful and obvious mechanism to build the continents Compared to the mass of the earth, the material that composes the continents is a very small fraction of the total. It is lighter than the other rock materials that make up the earth and is "floating" on top of the heavier materials. It probably did not start out as continental clumps, but started out separating from the other rocks "floating" up and spread out all over the earth under the oceans. In the beginning of the history of the earth, there may have been no continents.

But now there are continents. There are vast areas of continent surrounded by much greater areas of sea floor. The areas of sea floor cover over two-thirds of the globe. Most of the continental areas are within a few feet of sea level. Sea level is approximately three miles above the average sea floor level. To put that in perspective, very few of the highest mountains rise over three miles above sea level. In other words, the continents are vast plateau like areas rising three miles, over fifteen thousand feet, above average sea floor level.

What prevents time from taking it's toll and the plateau like areas of continents from slumping down and spreading out over the entire ocean floor?

Those questions have continued to be in my mind until just recently I heard of something that spurred a series of ideas in my mind. I heard of a deeply subducted solid piece of ocean floor plate somewhere under the west coast of the Americas. It was too deep to have arrived in that position by the slow rate of subduction observed by scientists today and to be still unmelted. Putting that piece of information together with many other observations I was able to come up with a theory to explain many of my unanswered questions, the greatest of which was why the continents are clumps sticking out of the ocean rather than scattered over the ocean floor under the water. In other words, the theory explains a possible mechanism for the formerly unexplained "mountain building episodes".

THE THEORY OF THE LITHOLOGIC CYCLE

This book presents the long missing mechanism responsible for the gathering together of the sialic rocks into continents. It is a new theory combining earth moving mechanisms together into The Theory of the Lithologic Cycle. The Lithologic Cycle has been in operation since the cooling of the earth reached the point of the earth having a solid crust overlaying liquid rock below.

The Theory of the Lithologic Cycle explains the balance where the continental rock material is kept gathered into continents as it is seen today.

In the Lithologic Cycle rock material is transported by three different mechanisms. They are erosion, subduction, and uplift. Water is the conveyor that carries the rock material from the continent and spreads it on the sea floor. Subducting sea floor is the conveyor that carries the rock material back to and under the continent. Isostacy is the elevator that lifts the rock again to the top of the mountains.

The erosion of the Hydrologic Cycle is only a part of the Lithologic Cycle. The Hydrologic Cycle is a cycle of nature that has been known and studied by scientists for years. The Hydrologic cycle is where ocean water is evaporated, carried by clouds over the land, rains on the land, runs off the land and returns back into the ocean where it began and the cycle begins over again. The hydrologic cycle spreads the continents out by its side effect of erosion. The erosion of the Hydrologic Cycle only explains the spreading of the continental rock material out to sea. The complete Lithologic Cycle furnishes the mechanisms to gather that spread material and to build the continents back up.

Runaway subduction is the heart of The Theory of the Lithologic Cycle. It is the periodic rapid sideways slide towards a continental plateau as the unstable ocean floor turns downward and rapidly sinks into the liquid below. This is the rapid turnover phase of the Lithologic cycle. This runaway subduction is necessary to explain the deep deposition of sialic material at the roots of mountain ranges. This is the key to the mountain building episodes of the past.

The theory of the Lithologic Cycle provides the answer to many questions concerning the origin and maintenance of the continents. These are questions which until now have remained unanswered. Implications of the theory of the Lithologic Cycle also pose many other questions concerning the interpretation of the geologic column, the geologic history of our world, fossil preservation and interpretation, mass extinctions and renewal of ecological balance, and the ruggedness of the ecological adaptation to extreme disruptions. The geologic record shows several repetitions of some disruption in the balance of the crust of the earth. There are at least five major mass extinction and ecological recovery episodes recorded in the fossil record. These are probably due to the rapid turnover phase of the Lithologic Cycle. This suggests that the isostatic balance in the crust of the earth is much more fragile than the ecological balance.

PHASES OF THE LITHOLOGIC CYCLE

There are four phases of the Lithologic Cycle. In chronological order, they are the Isostatic Balance Phase, the Trigger Phase, The Rapid Turnover Phase, and the Isostatic Rebound Phase.

We are current living in the Isostatic Balance Phase. Isostatic balance is where the weight of a vertical column of mass of one horizontal area is the same as any other equal size horizontal area. The mountains are less dense and therefore rise higher in the mantle. The ocean floor is more dense and therefore sinks lower into mantle. The Isostatic Balance Phase is a relatively long period of time compared to the other phases.

Currently the other three phases occur in a rapid succession of events. That rapid succession of events occurs in an extremely small amount of time compared to the duration of the Isostatic Balance Phase. The geologic record indicates many repetitions of the Lithologic Cycle since the beginning of life on this planet.

The Trigger Phase is the phase that starts the rapid succession of events. It could be the slow gradual build up of stress and deformation rate that causes the trigger. It could be some outside force such as a meteor impact that releases the strain. In different repetitions of the Lithologic Cycle it may be a different mechanism that is the trigger. In any event the result is the beginning of the Rapid Turnover Phase. The trigger must be big enough to break loose the contact between the plates along the complete front such that other parts of the plate contact would not be able to hold the strain and stop the turnover.

The Rapid Turnover Phase relieves the strain that is built up during the long duration of the Isostatic Balance Phase. The Rapid Turnover Phase is an event best described as runaway subduction where the old ocean floor rapidly sinks into the mantle below in an avalanche type event. This generally occurs at the edge of a continent with the old ocean floor moving toward the continent in the same direction as the slow subduction seen during the Isostatic Balance Phase. The runaway subduction continues until either the strain is relieved and inertia drives the plates no further and the speed again returns to a slow creep, or until something jams preventing any further relief of strain. The maximum duration of this phase is on the order of magnitude of a month. Any slower movement of the runaway would allow the sliding surfaces to again lock down to creep speed.

The Rapid Turnover Phase is the ultimate "Big One" in the context of earthquakes. As the study of earthquakes continues we realize that the major cause of earthquakes is an acceleration in the subduction of crustal plates caused by the same mechanisms which drive the Lithologic Cycle. The earthquakes that we frequently observe and experience have a practical upper limit of earth movement. That upper limit is the complete turnover of the ocean floor. Such an event would have a duration on the order of a month and would be the ultimate "Big One": a rapid turnover phase of the Lithologic Cycle.

The Isostatic Rebound Phase occurs immediately after the Rapid Turnover Phase and may occur in multiple parts. The first part may be during the dying out of the waves set up in the mantle by the catastrophic earthquake event. Another part may be the rising of the sialic material drug down by the rubbing of the upper surface of the subducting plate against the continent. Yet a third part may be the sinking of the new ocean floor as it cools, again allowing the ocean to return into it's basins.

Some of the characteristics that define each of the phases are listed in the table below along with some of the side effects which generate evidence of the occurrence of the event.

Phases:

Isostatic Balance Phase (Long time duration)
 Current time in history
 Horizontal isostatic balance
 Vertical instability grows to critical

Trigger phase
 Spontaneous with buildup of stress or
 Triggered by outside event such as
  Meteorite impact
  Near approach other celestial object, etc.

Rapid turnover phase (Very short time- few days to months)
 Rapid ocean floor sinking.
 Runaway subduction at continental edge.
  pulls edge of continent down
  conveyor action deposits sial under continents
  stretching, overturning & doubling of continental edge
 Mid ocean ridge may temporarily rise above sea level
  rapid ocean floor rise at mid ocean
   rise beyond isostatic balance point
   result of wave or inertia from rapid subduction
  enable continuous spreading
  enable rapid simultaneous movement of continents
  avert rapid quench
  temporary displacement of oceans onto continents.
 Quenching new ocean floor raises temperature of ocean
  mass extinction in ocean

increased evaporation causes increased precipitation.
worldwide flooding with mass extinction
enables rapid burial and preservation of fossils
New ocean floor hotter, less dense is isostatically higher
Higher sea level floods continents
mass extinction on continents
massive erosion & sedimentation
rapid burial and fossilization of remains
preserves record of life before mass extinction
Deep mantle effects
cooling surface of core
rapid convection in core
rapid magnetic reversals due to rapid convection

Isostatic Rebound phase
Mountain building episode
new deposits below continents lift continents higher
Ocean floor lowering
Water gathering again into the ocean basins.

BASIS OF THE THEORY OF THE LITHOLOGIC CYCLE

There are two major types of rocks that make up the surface of the earth. The continental rocks are primarily sialic. Sialic is a word standing for Silicon (Si) and Aluminum (Al) referring to the major ingredients in these rocks. The ocean floor rocks are primarily mafic. Mafic is a word standing for Magnesium (Mg) and Iron (Fe) referring to the major ingredients of these rocks. Sialic rocks have a specific gravity of approximately 2.6 to 2.7. Mafic rocks have a specific gravity of approximately 3.2. Solidified rocks of both kinds have a slightly higher specific gravity than the melted rock of the same kind.

Sial is by far the more scarce of the two rock types even though the continents are almost exclusively made of Sial. Mafic rock is much more abundant. The ocean floor is Mafic. The rock below the sial of the continents is mafic. The continents can be visualized as islands of sial floating in a sea of mafic rock. The surface may appear to be solid, but the rock below is virtually molten.

The lighter solidified Sial gathered together into the continents is actually floating on top of the more plentiful heavier type of rock below. The heavier solidified Mafic ocean floor lies along side the Sial of the continent, sunken much lower into the liquid below. It is isostatically pressed into the molten rock below, and is not actually floating because it is more dense than the molten rock below it. The sialic rock type of the continents is underlain by the more plentiful and more dense Mafic rock type. This is a stable condition. The more dense mafic type rock of the floor of the ocean basins is resting on molten rock of the same type. The molten rock below is less dense than the solid rock above and has the tendency to rise as the more dense rock above tends to sink. This is an unstable condition and therein lies the key to the mechanism that has gathered the Sial into continents and has built the mountains of the Sial.

The dynamics of the Lithologic Cycle is driven by these simple facts: The solid continental rocks are less dense than the liquid rock in which they are floating. The solid ocean floor rock is more dense than the liquid rock beneath. The ocean floor is not floating, but is bridged across in an unstable way. Solid ocean floor rock continuously creeps and then periodically slides rapidly sideways towards a continental plateau as it turns downward and rapidly sinks into the liquid below. This generally results in what is called an earthquake. At the upper limit of magnitude of earth movement during such an earthquake is the theoretical runaway subduction of the Lithologic Cycle Theory.

EFFECTS PREDICTED BY THE THEORY

The Lithologic Cycle has a long stable time where the ocean level is relatively stable as the ocean floor rock is relatively cool and solid. During this time the mountains are wearing down by erosion and the old solid ocean floor which slid off into the hot liquid is slowly warming up and melting. During this current phase of the cycle evidence of the last time the rapid turnover phase hit has begun to fade away. Man has developed theories that things always were as they are now. There are a few nagging questions like where did the mountains come from, but even most scientists are content to live with not knowing everything. However, this is an unstable situation as the old ocean floor melts the situation gets even more unstable, until some event such as a large meteorite or comet comes near or collides with the earth touching off yet another rapid turnover phase.

The rapid turnover phase begins with the old heavy ocean floor rapidly sliding off toward the middle of the earth into the liquid below. This probably occurs over a time period on the order of a month. The speed of the sliding could be described as a fast jog, a few miles per hour.
Accompanying the sinking of the ocean floor are many other phenomena. There is subduction of the edge of the continent which normally is floating in a stable balance in the liquid because of it's lighter rock type. The sinking of the ocean floor rock drags the continental rocks down with it due to friction. New hot liquid rock rises in mid ocean as the old sea floor slides sideways, That new hot liquid rock solidifies to take it's place in a band along and parallel to the trailing edge of the sliding sinking sheet of rock. This new rock is hotter and therefore lighter so it does not press down into the surface as deeply as the old ocean floor and therefore the new ocean floor is higher and sea level rises covering much, if not all of the continental rocks, depending on the subduction effect. In addition there may be additional rising of the mid ocean due to upwelling of the convection in response to the sinking of the old cold rock of the ocean floor a few thousand miles away. Such massive disturbances in the crust of the earth may possibly even be accompanied by massive tidal waves in the liquid rock of the mantle analogous to the tidal waves on the ocean water accompanying the disturbance of surface earthquakes.

Simultaneously with the subduction of one side of the continental mass, a few thousand miles away in the opposite direction from the ocean, the surface of the earth may split down the middle of a supercontinent from the tension and convectional upwelling. Hot molten rock wells up into this secondary split, thus tilting the whole continental mass in between. In the tilted situation, the continental mass then slides rapidly, like a surfer on a wave, away from the secondary split toward the area of subduction leaving behind a vast area of the earth surface covered by the material of which ocean floor is made. (The Atlantic Ocean appears to be the result of this secondary split during a recent repetition of the Lithologic Cycle.) Let me say it again. The time span of this rapid turnover phase of the Lithologic Cycle may be on the order of a month. In a very short time a continent may be moved a great distance on the surface of the earth with sudden drastic and permanent changes of climate.

This rapid renewal of the ocean floor with hot liquid rock has two immediate effects. First, the hotter rock of the new ocean floor is less dense and in a much thinner layer than previously. This causes the ocean floor to be in isostatic balance at a much higher level than previously. This causes the ocean to spread out over the continental rocks resulting in a lesser water load of weight over the ocean floor and a greater load of weight over the continents, further depressing the continents relative to the ocean floor areas. Much, if not virtually all the continental areas are covered with ocean water for a short time until the new ocean floor cools and sinks to a depth allowing the ocean to return. Second, The new hot ocean floor heats the ocean water, especially at the contact between sea water and molten rock where there is boiling of the sea. This causes torrential rainfall over the whole earth. The torrential rainfall, flooding and washing over of the continents, along with the worldwide massive earthquakes causes massive habitat destruction and massive erosion resulting in a tremendous layer of sediment containing massive fossils due to the rapid burial and subsequent preservation. Just a side note, the geologic record may be a series of such layers, a record of the Lithologic Cycles.

As the old ocean floor sinks into the liquid below, the mechanism that generates the magnetic field of the earth is disrupted. By some mechanism, the irregularities of the sinking of the cold rock or the rapid convection in the liquid portion of the core, causes rapid reversals in the earth's magnetic field. Magnetic field reversals are recorded in the stripes of solidified lava which make up the current ocean floors.

It appears that during a recent Lithologic Cycle ocean floor turnover, the secondary split was between the current continents of Europe/Africa, and North/South America, with North and South America sliding over the sinking Pacific ocean floor due to subduction on the west edge and rising hot lava rock to the east. Previous episodes (or maybe even the last one) of the rapid turnover phase may be responsible for some of the areas where continents appear to have collided causing high mountain ranges such as the Himalayas.

The rebound phase of the Lithologic Cycle is where the new ocean floor cools and presses itself deeper into the liquid below allowing the ocean water to again run off the continental land masses back into the ocean basins. During this rebound phase the mountain building occurs and new Geomorphologically related topography develops. Lighter low density continental rock material drug down by subduction, rebound to be in balance as it is floating in the hot liquid rock below. Rock that has been newly drug down under the old continental rocks increase the thickness of the continental rocks and therefore rebound to a greater elevation.   Thus is the discovery of the long sought after mechanism required to explain mountain building and the appearance of mountain building to be episodic.

SOME DETAILS OF THE THEORY OF THE LITHOLOGIC CYCLEInstabilities in the Structure of the Earth's Crust

Let's look at what really exists now. There is a big difference between the ocean area and the continental area. The continent is typically about 15 miles of lighter (less dense) rock floating over the medium density, less solid mantle. The ocean floor is typically about three miles of water over about five miles of heavier (more dense) solid crustal rock over medium density, less solid hot mantle. The two different columns of earth surface material are shown side by side in the figure of typical columns of earth crust in balance.

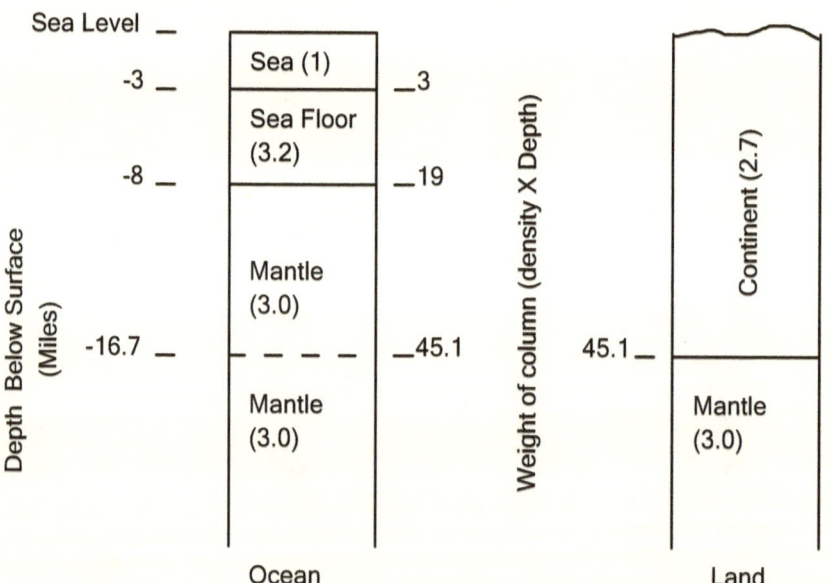

Typical Columns of Earth Crust in Balance (Isostacy)

This balance is called isostacy. Height of each column adjusts itself vertically so the total weight is the same at the lower end of the column. The sea floor, being made of heavier rock, generally lies some three miles lower than sea level. The continental rocks on the other hand, are lighter, and generally stick up a fraction of a mile above sea level. The thicker the layer of continental rocks, the deeper they sink into the mantle and the higher they stick up as mountains, always keeping in balance with the ocean column and the column of surrounding continental rocks. When something happens to get the columns out of balance, the continental columns rise or lower to remain in balance.

Our quest is to find out what mechanism it is that causes the columns to get out of balance. It is this out of balance state that causes the mountains to rise taking sea level deposited sedimentary rock to great heights in a mountain building episode. We know this occurs because without periodic uplifting, the mountains would erode and be washed out to sea. We know this occurs because we see sedimentary rocks with fossils of sea creatures at great heights in the mountains.

There are two sources of potential energy in the columns that are obvious sources of energy to drive the imbalance. The first is the part of the continental rocks that stick up above the level of the sea floor. This potential energy drives the spreading of the continents sideways to displace the lighter water. The second is the density inversion in the ocean column where the more dense solid crustal ocean floor is over the less dense, more fluid mantle.

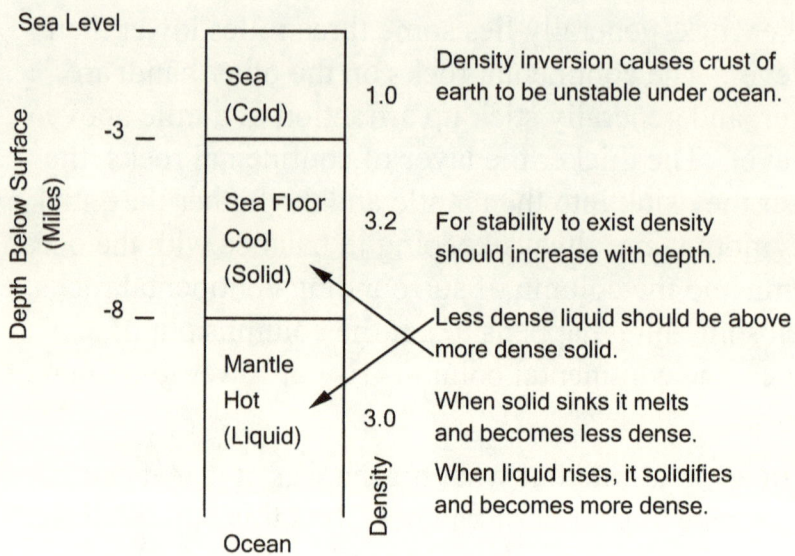

Typical Column of Earth Crust With Density Inversion
(Simplified)

This density inversion in the ocean column is due to the fact that when rock cools and solidifies, it shrinks. When rock shrinks, it is more dense. The same amount of weight is in a smaller space. When water freezes to ice, the opposite effect takes place. Water expands when it becomes ice. The lighter ice floats on top of the water. That is why icebergs float instead of sinking. That is why a pond will develop a layer of ice over the surface in cold weather. If the ice were more dense than the water, it would sink and a lake would accumulate ice from the bottom up. Rock is the opposite of water. Solidified rock will sink in hot liquid rock.

This force tending to make the ocean floor sink into the mantle is tremendous. The density of the solid rock of the ocean floor is approximately 3.2. That is about 3.2 times the density of pure water. The density of the mantle is approximately 3.0. That is about 0.2 difference. If the ocean floor crust is about five miles thick, that is five miles times the 0.2 difference in density. or 1.0. This is equivalent to the weight of a column of water one mile high. That is a lot of pressure pressing the crust into the mantle. That estimate is on the order of magnitude of 150 tons for every square foot of ocean floor. If the ocean floor crust is solid for a thicker layer than that in the illustration, then the magnitude of the differential pressure is proportionally greater depending on the thickness.

Then why doesn't the ocean floor sink? There are two answers. (1.) It would if the liquid mantle could flow out and over the solid crust. But, when it starts to, the cold and very heat conductive water of the ocean freezes it again to solid rock stopping the leak. (2.) It does. The ocean floor is sinking slowly by sliding under the continents at the rate of a few centimeters per year. That slow sinking is called subduction.

In subduction we have found a mechanism that tends to gather the lighter rocks into a continent. As the ocean floor slowly sinks under the continent, it moves from the middle of the ocean, the mid oceanic ridge area, toward the continent. As it moves toward the continent, it carries the sediment on it that has come from the erosion of the continent, back to the continent. This subduction carries the sediment back to the edge of the continent where it adds to the side of the continent as the subducting ocean floor slowly sinks under the edge of the continent.

But this slow continuous subduction does not solve our problem of the mountain building episodes. Currently the subduction is occurring, but the mountains are still eroding away faster than they are growing. We must find a way to hurry up the mountain building process. A significant speeding up of subduction could account for it, but this does not happen. Once subduction speeds up much more than it is now going, it breaks into earthquake speed for a few seconds. That is our first clue.

But first, lets play with the numbers of the balance of isostacy. For example, what would happen if there were one mile less depth of water in the ocean? Would the continents stick out one mile higher? No. The weight being removed from the ocean column would result in the ocean floor moving up the height of rock with weight equivalent to the mile of missing water. That would be about a third of a mile because rock is about that much more dense than water. The continents would then be sticking out of the water about two-thirds of a mile. That is still much higher than sea level and erosion would much more aggressively wear down the continents to approximately their same profile as we see them today. All this eroded material would add to the diameter of the continents. At that point the continents would have unloaded the weight of two thirds of a mile of rock. Having unloaded that weight, the continents would again rise isostatically, thus renewing the aggressiveness of the erosion, further increasing the diameter of the continents due to their reduced thickness. This equivalent reduction in the size of the oceans would increase the depth of the remaining ocean area until isostacy was again achieved and the size of the continents adjusted to achieve an ocean sea level relative to the surface of the continents similar to what we see today.

Again lets have some fun with the numbers. What if suddenly the ocean floor were solid only a few feet instead of about five miles. The increase in size of the rock accompanying the decrease in the density would cause isostacy to be accomplished with the ocean floor a third of a mile higher, relative to the continents, than it is now. With the majority of the continents surface being less than third of a mile in altitude above sea level, guess what? The ocean would spill over onto the continents. Two other effects would be in action. First, the weight of the additional water on the continents would weigh them down to a greater depth. Second, this sudden condition would only happen when there was a rapid runaway subduction, a sinking of the old ocean floor under the existing mountain chains. The inertia and friction of this rapid sinking on the order of a thousand miles, would surely cause the subduction of the mountains on the order of magnitude enough to bring them to sea level or below. This condition would only last a short time. The result would be an earth temporarily covered with water virtually worldwide.

When the rapid sinking stops, rebound of the mountains would occur. The mountain roots would be deeper due to the lighter erosional material from the weathering of the top of the mountains being drug under the mountains by the rapid runaway subduction. Thus the mountains would grow to greater heights. Thus the missing mechanism for mountain building is found. As the crust of the sea floor quickly cools and shrinks, it would again come to rest at or near it's original balance height. As a result, the water would flow back into the ocean basins, again achieving the normal sea levels and isostatic balance.

Flash Liquefaction and Earthquakes

In the context of earthquakes, subduction, and continental drift, solid rocks which are tightly pressed together slide relative to each other. The rate of movement has been observed to be primarily either very slow, or quite rapid, the difference between the two rates being on the order of nine orders of magnitude. These speeds I call creep speed and earthquake speed. Creep speed is on the order of magnitude of a few centimeters per year. Earthquake speed is on the order of a few miles per hour, possibly best illustrated as a fast jog. The difference between the two speeds is a factor on the order of magnitude of 1,000,000,000, a billion. Earthquake speed is on the order of a billion times faster than creep speed. Rock movement in the surface of the earth has been observed at these two speeds, almost universally, but not much movement (if any) has been recorded at speeds in between. When the rock movement between large plates of rock shifts from creep speed to earthquake speed and back to creep speed(or stopped), shock waves are sent out from the location of the speed change and we record the event as an earthquake. Thousands of earthquakes are recorded each year. When we see continents moving at creep speed we call it Continental Drift. The drifting continents have been mapped worldwide. Movement along major faults such as the famous San Andreas, active in the great San Francisco earthquake of 1906, has been observed to be at creep speed for several decades now with occasional shifts to earthquake speed and back to creep speed with an accompanying earthquake.

There is a difference between sliding and static friction, especially when the two surfaces are being firmly pressed together. There are various different reasons for this, but it is a generally true physical phenomena. To illustrate this physical phenomena to yourself, be sure your hands are dry and free of any oil or lotion. Press your open hands lightly together and slowly slide them back and forth in a lightly rubbing motion. Now increase the pressure pushing your hands together and notice that the smooth slow motion becomes a series of jerky slips. In applying this general principle to rocks, these jerky slips are earthquake speed, and the times between are the imperceptible movement of creep speed. In the context of snow, such speed changes are called avalanche.

What is an earthquake? The deformation rate of the rock in the process of subduction occurs over a long time and is slow. It is called creep. Creep is microscopic deformation of the rock and on the large scale is imperceptible from moment to moment. Over the long time it is obvious it has happened because the rocks are not where they were. As the slow creep becomes faster, as the deformation rate exceeds the microscopic creep limit, there is suddenly an acceleration. The rate of movement increases by approximately 9 orders of magnitude. The speed of a few centimeters per year becomes a few miles per hour. Then, just as suddenly, when the built up strain is released, the deceleration is just as abrupt. This results in an earthquake as the shock waves of the acceleration and deceleration radiate out from the point of acceleration and deceleration.

Why does this creep rate have a limit beyond which there is sudden acceleration? The answer may be found in a phenomena that occurs in rocks, flash liquefaction. When rocks are under strain and tremendous pressure, as molecular deformation rate increases, the contact material becomes more like a fluid on the microscopic level. As it becomes more like a fluid the deformation rate increases due the more fluid rock acting more like a lubricant. This is positive feedback until it reaches a certain point and results in runaway acceleration. Once the rock is moving at the high speed on the order of magnitude of a few miles per hour it quickly relieves the strain, possibly even driven past the point of strain relief by the inertia of the moving rock. With the driving force of strain being relieved, the rock quickly slows down then just as suddenly decelerates as the liquefaction reverts back to solid. This rock that went through the liquefaction and back, is left as evidence. It is what geologists call "slickensides" and is commonly found in faults that have had earthquakes.

Again lets call upon ice and water to get an understanding of what this flash liquefaction can do. After people have ice skated on the surface of ice, there is a trail that looks like a scratch in the ice. It is not a scratch, but is the evidence of the ice suddenly turning to liquid, lubricating the skate as it passes over, then just as suddenly turning back to solid. It is analogous to slickensides in a fault zone. When an ice skate is stationary, not moving at all, it can freeze to the ice. A little effort will not move the skate. If you slowly increase the force applied to start the skate, suddenly it moves and continues to move almost effortlessly. That is the same phenomena of flash liquefaction lubricating two differentially moving surfaces.

Flash Liquefaction and Runaway Subduction

This brings us to the big step in the thought process developing the theory of The Lithologic Cycle. The big thought stimulant that seems significant to me is the subducted ocean floor under the west coast of the Americas. Seismic tomography, the science of mapping the interior of the earth by seismic wave propagation has revealed plates of unmelted sea floor far beneath the continent, too far to be still there if it melts back into mantle material as it subducts at the current rate. If that is true, there must be some explanation of how it got there so rapidly. Even if it is not true, the thought exercise has resulted in a valid hypothesis which will be subjected to the test of time.

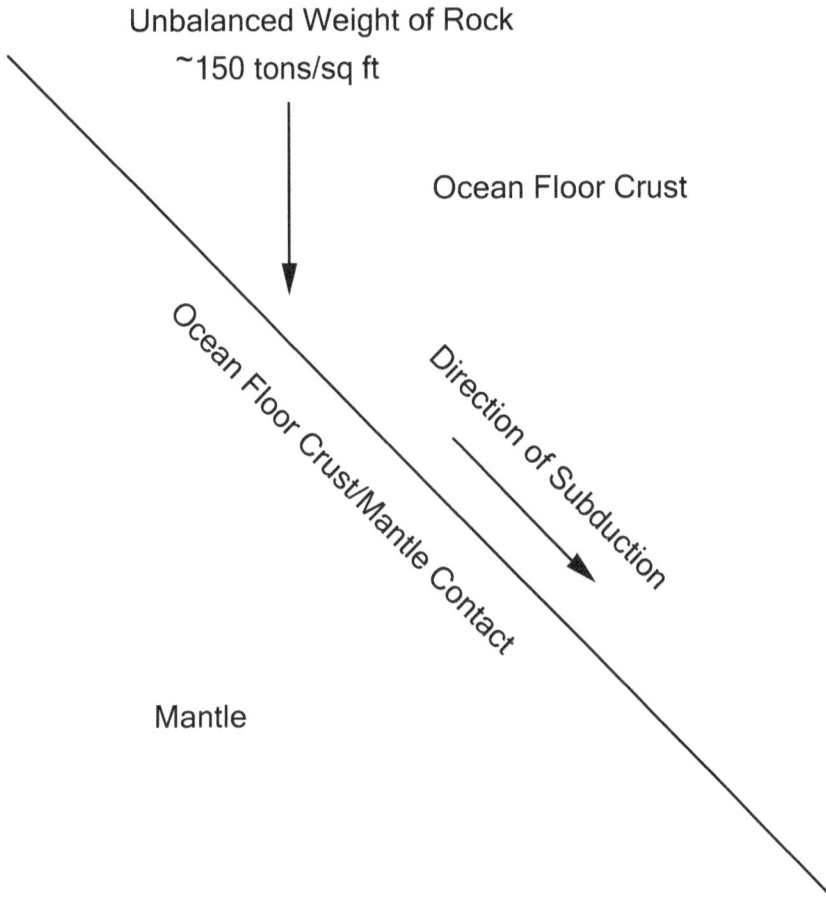

A possible mechanism for runaway subduction would be the tremendous pressure tending to cause the ocean floor to sink into the mantle, and flash liquefaction (or whatever the release mechanism is) resulting in the same phenomena as an earthquake, but one that did not stop until the entire ocean floor sank into the mantle. Whether this turnover was spontaneous, or triggered by some external event such as a meteorite impact is immaterial. The important fact is that the rocks have told the geologists that there are mountain building episodes and this is a possible explanation of the missing mechanism. The accompanying effects of such an event would give precisely what geologists would call evidence of a mountain building episode.

HISTORICAL PROGRESSION OF THE LITHOLOGIC CYCLE

If the earth at one stage of it's development, had been much hotter internally than it is now, it would have had a much thinner crust. When it was hot enough to have a crust a few inched to a few feet thick, sinking of chunks of solid into the liquid below would have been a daily occurrence. The heavier solidified crust would sink into the liquid below and more liquid rock would take its place and cool to become solid. As the crust sank, it would not just settle down, but slide off to one side and slip vertically into the liquid below the surface. As each piece sank, it would turn up on edge as it sank so it could sink more rapidly through the viscous liquid. As the earth cooled the thickness of the solid crust would increase and the breaking off and sinking would occur less often and in bigger chunks. At some stage of the cooling, the water layer would develop such that the entire earth may have been at one time completely covered with water if this occurred before the continents developed. The water layer helped in the rapid cooling of the crust uniformly around the surface of the earth. Since the Sialic substance is less dense than the Mafic, there would be a separation of the Sialic and Mafic rocks such that the section of crust that sank would have more of a concentration of Sial in the top side. After the sinking and standing vertically, one side would have a higher concentration of the lighter rock and the other side a higher concentration of the heavier rock. As each chunk sank into the hot liquid below, it would remelt. As it remelted in a vertical position, a pool of sial would float to the surface. The rising of the sial would thus be gathered together into small areas on the surface of the crust. Thus, islands of Sial formed in the sea of Mafic

rock. As the Sialic islands grew, there was a tendency for
the sinking of the Mafic crust to be toward the Sialic
islands as this was the lowest areas due to the depression
left when the last slab of floor sank. Such a depression is
analogous to the deep trench at the edges of the Pacific
Ocean where the ocean floor is currently subducting below
the continents. The rising of the sial would thus be
gathered together into small areas on the surface of the
crust. These small areas would then become pre-
continents. As the pre-continents became more massive
due to repeatedly receiving loads of sial from sinking
crust, the pre-continents would float higher in the molten
rock below than the level of the surrounding mafic crust.
Isostacy, the balance of height of objects supported in a
fluid dictates the lower density areas have a higher surface
elevation than the higher density areas. Many repetitions
of this cycle resulted in the continents emerging above the
level of the ocean water and the environment to sustain
life on the continents developed.

Early stages

See above

Middle stages

Emergence of continent(s)
Continents grow from their roots. Sedimentary surface rocks
deposition increased during massive flooding. Volcanic
surface rocks deposited by volcanism, maybe increased
during subduction or rebound phases.

Life on continents.

Repeated Mass extinctions and Re-development of balanced ecology

Recent stages

Rapid turnover and isostatic rebound triggered by Meteor impact?

Current stage

Semi stable. Instability due to potential energy of density inversion

Future stages

> Meteor impact or spontaneous runaway triggers rapid
> > turnover
> Earthquake and flood causes destruction, extinction, and
> > preservation
> > Relentless earthquakes rupture fuel distribution systems
> > Coastal and lowland cities destroyed by fire then flood
> > Massive flooding and erosion bury and preserve remains
> Isostatic rebound
> Ecological recovery

Obvious conclusion: The solid crust of the earth itself is less sturdy than Ecology.

The Maturing of the Cycle

At first the periodic sinking of the crust was not such a major event. The crust probably was not very thick and the resistance of pieces of the crust to slide relative to one another was hardly a factor. Pieces of the crust would just break off and sink. Periodically the ocean floor sank below the edge of the continent. As the continents grew, and the thickness of the crust that sank increased due to the cooling of the earth due to this turning over of the crust. As the thickness of the sinking slab increased, the scale of the convulsion increased. As the scale of the convulsion increased, the time between convulsions increased.

Now here is the key to the present status of the Lithologic Cycle. The sinking of the crustal slab does not occur at the slow creeping speed of what we now observe as continental drift, but at the faster (by nine orders of magnitude) earthquake speed. The speed that rocks move when the motion is detected as an earthquake is fast enough that the entire ocean floor could slide under the continent in about a month. This rapid speed of the sinking crustal slab would cause the sinking slab to drag part of the edge of the continent down with it thus making the continent have less spread and more depth. After the movement stopped, in the rebound phase of the cycle the mass of sial that was drug down would float upward, adding to the root of the mountains, thus lifting the mountains to greater height.

SUPPORTING EVIDENCE AND OBSERVATIONS

There is much evidence that his cycle has continued to the present. This evidence is seen in current observations and is recorded in the rocks of the geologic column, and in our written historical accounts passed down to us from ancient times. The continents exist. The laws of physics dictate instability due to vertical density inversions. The geologic record shows sea floor spreading, continental drift, and a young ocean floor. The geologic record shows episodic mountain building periods with long quiet periods between. The geologic record shows less diversity of life forms after each mountain building episode. The geologic record shows abrupt changes where up to 90% of all species on earth became extinct. The widespread impact craters dominating the landscape of the moon are nearly absent on Earth. Seismic tomography indicates the presence of a slab of old Pacific Ocean floor, newly sunken and still unmelted below the west side of the Americas. Archaeological records predicted by the theory of evolution are missing. Recorded history abruptly begins too recently with several fully developed written languages, Nearly very culture has a legend of an ancient flood with their ancestors as the sole survivors. There is an absence of widespread human graves or fossil remains older than the flood legends. The evidence of a recent repetition of the cycle is overwhelming:

The continents exist. Just the fact that the continents are sticking out above the water in defiance of erosion and gravity is amazing. In the absence of a counter mechanism, the continental rocks should be spread out in a layer surrounding the earth. That layer should be about five miles thick, over the mantle, and under the water of the oceans. The fact that the continental rocks are gathered into piles over three times that thick is evidence of the effect of some forceful mechanism at work. The fact that the top of the continents are above water, standing up over three miles above the ocean floor is evidence that the Lithologic Cycle continues to function.

The laws of physics dictate vertical crustal instability due to vertical density inversions.

Physics of isostatic balance, the difference in vertical elevation between the ocean floor and the continental plateau's, and the weakness of the material making up the continents dictate horizontal crustal instability.

The geologic record shows sea floor spreading, continental drift, and a young ocean floor. Geologists have no practical mechanism assigned to this.

The geologic record shows episodic mountain building periods with relative long quiet periods between. Geologists have no practical mechanism assigned to this phenomena.

The geologic fossil record shows less diversity of life forms after each mountain building episode.

The geologic fossil record shows abrupt changes where up to 90% of all species on earth became extinct. These abrupt changes have been called mass extinctions. A mass extinction is when a significant number of the species on the earth become extinct in a short period of time due to a common cause.

The widespread impact craters dominating the landscape of the moon are nearly absent on the earth. It is not that they never happened. They have been erased by the renewal of the surface. The erosion of the hydrologic cycle and the maintenance of the continents by the Lithologic Cycle are the dominating factors determining the landscape of the continents.

Seismic tomography indicates the presence of a slab of old Pacific Ocean floor, newly sunken and still unmelted below the west side of the Americas.

Archaeological records predicted by the theory of evolution are missing. Widespread archaeological remains record the existence of man on this earth only a few thousand years. Before that the archaeological remains are suddenly meager if any. The Theory of Evolution predicts the existence of man on earth being at least ten times as long as the widespread archaeological remains record. This number times the number of different areas on earth in which human cultures could develop preclude the possibility that there could be no ancient civilization predating our historical and archaeological record. The postulation that modern man meagerly existed for ninety thousand years then suddenly burst forth with complicated civilization and technology in a very short time nearly ten thousand years ago is ludicrous. The theory of evolution therefore requires a destruction of the archaeological record by something like the rapid turnover phase of the Lithologic Cycle..

Recorded history is available only a few thousand years back. Recorded history abruptly begins too recently with several fully developed written languages.

Nearly every culture has a legend of an ancient flood with their ancestors as the sole survivors.

There is an absence of widespread human graves or fossil remains older than the flood legends.

QUESTIONS TO BE EXPLORED

Was the earth once as the stable picture painted above then some perturbation such as a meteor impact cause the mantle to be exposed and then start the Lithologic Cycle?

Why is the ocean floor higher in the middle from an isostacy viewpoint?

Why is there a magnetic field and what is it's relationship to subduction, etc. Does the relationship have anything to do with magnetic field declining or pole wandering?

Does magnetic field decline as the source of cold warms up and the convection slows?

Are apparent reversals in magnetic field due to change in relative motion as the old ocean floor slides under the continent at runaway speeds?

Are apparent reversals in magnetic field due to rapid convection of the liquid portion of the core of the earth due to a cold slab of ocean crust cooling a portion of the surface of that liquid core?

Why is ocean floor drift toward continent?

Why is the sial gathered into continents over only a fraction of the earth's surface instead of spread over the entire surface of the earth?

In the stable phase of the Lithologic Cycle, it seems logical that the roots of mountains would erode as do the upper side tending to spread the sial over the surface of the earth.

Why does the gathering of the sial (the mountain building) occur intermittently instead of constantly as does the erosion? These times have been referred to by geologists as "mountain building episodes". If the gathering is due to long term creep speed subduction it should be in balance with erosion, not episodic.

The Fragile Earth. The fragility is in the solid crust, not the ecology.

Could an alternate explanation of the source of the sial be from a meteor itself rather than from density separation from the mantle?

IMPLICATIONS OF THE THEORY OF THE LITHOLOGIC CYCLE

The solid rock of the crust is more fragile than the ecology The earth is fragile, not life on the earth as we have been led to religiously believe, but the crust of the earth itself. The geologic record shows that the ecology has been drastically disrupted many times over, yet life continues and the ecological balance returns. The continents themselves suffer inundation, the sea floor sinks rapidly into the depths of the earth, the extinction of the majority of the species on earth wipes out life on earth as it is before the convulsion. Yet, life survives and ecological balance returns with the surviving species. The effect of man on the earth and its ecology is negligible relative to what the earth does to itself. What we have been led to believe is not always as it seems. The ecology is fragile, but the crust of the earth which supports the ecology is as stable as a rock, or so we are lead to believe in basic grade school science class. However, more and more we are coming to the undeniable conclusion that the ecology has suffered massive disruptions and always brings itself back into balance. It is the crust of the earth that is fragile. Major disruptions of the ecology due to catastrophic convulsions of the crust are the rule rather than the exception.

Mountain Building Episodes and Mass Extinctions

I have observed over the past 30 years that geology has turned from looking for continuity of evolution to describing the fossil record as a series of mass extinctions. This theoretical cycle as I have described predicts the geologic record should contain mountain building episodes with mass extinctions including rapid burial of large animal remains. Nowhere on earth at present do we see massive large animal burial and preservation occurring. This should only occur during the relative short time of the upheaval phase of the mountain building cycle giving a snapshot record of life on earth just prior to the mass extinction. The geologic record should show species to be a series of rapid appearance and rapid extinctions rather than a continuous development of life on earth. This Lithologic Cycle Theory fits both the model of surviving species rapidly adapting to the new environment (ecology) after a mass extinction and the model of punctuated evolution. Rapid development of the human race overtaking and dominating the earth during the past 10,000 years would be an example of surviving species adaptation.

Currently the most popular hypothesis explaining the mass extinction of the Dinosaurs is a huge meteor impacting the earth and the following global warming and greenhouse effect. This hypothesis is inadequate in that it does not explain the universal rapid burial and preservation of the large animal remains. A better hypothesis is the meteor impact was sufficient to deform the fragile crust of the earth triggering a rapid turnover phase of the Lithologic Cycle which included mass extinction due to massive flood and rapid burial of large animal remains due to massive erosion during the flooding and ensuing runoff. If this all happened in the time frame on the order of magnitude of a single year it would explain the preservation of the remains which would otherwise be picked apart by scavengers and decomposed by exposure. It would also explain why the birds and other small animals escaped extinction.

Would the mass extinctions described in the Scientific American Magazine be better described as snapshots of life on earth captured by the massive flooding, erosion and fossil preservation of a rapid turnover phase of the Lithologic Cycle? After each mass extinction is a lapse of record. Could this be the long isostatic balance phase where few fossils are preserved and the ecology recovers and is then captured again and again in the fossil record of subsequent rapid turnover events?

The mass extinctions of the distant past are probably due to the fragileness of the crust, not the fragileness of ecology. The record of the distant past shows many times the ecology was destroyed resulting in mass extinctions. It also shows just as many recoveries due to the forces that bring the ecology back into balance in spite of the destructions.

It is typical for a scientist to do research looking for one thing and end up discovering something completely different. When I was going to school studying geology, geologists were looking for fossils to fill in a complete picture of continuous evolution from simple to complex. Now the reports are coming in of the findings of the search resulting in a picture of disjointed snapshots of various ecologies of the past where the abundance of species is dwindling. Mass extinctions interspersed with long periods of lack of fossil record of the ecological recovery are painting a picture of the lack of Uniformitarianism in the distant past.

The Sedimentary Geologic Column and the Lithologic Cycle

It has long been recognized that the sedimentary geologic column is not a record of continuous deposition. All geologists recognize that the geologic column in any one locality is a record of a series of depositions interspersed with discontinuities. A deposition is the record of a period of time when the surface of the earth at that point was below water and was the area where the products of erosion were deposited A discontinuity is the record of a period of time when the surface of the rock was above water and was being eroded.

Prior to the recognition of the Lithologic Cycle, it was assumed that the mountains of the continents slowly moved up and down at the rates observed in recent times. The mechanism driving these up and down cycles has never been adequately explained. However, their necessity has been dictated by the fact of the existence of the series of depositions and discontinuities. It has been assumed that the deposition had to be slow, because the current vertical motion of the continents is almost imperceptibly slow. The problem with the slow deposition theory is that fossils are preserved by rapid burial. With slow deposition, the remains that are fossilized, would have been destroyed by weathering before being buried at the slow deposition rate and could not have been preserved as we see them today. The only explanation scientists had to offer is the deposition at times had to be rapid and episodic.

The sedimentary geologic column is a record of many episodes of continental flooding, of deposition and fossil preservation interspersed with discontinuities. In many areas the geologic column may be reinterpreted as a series of snapshots of life on that part of the earth just prior to mass extinctions interspersed with long periods of time where a new ecology develops from the remaining species adapting to the new environment. This is in fact what is predicted by the Lithologic Cycle theory of continental building.

The Lithologic Cycle and the Theory of the Evolution of Man

It is not the purpose of this book to support or refute any theory, religion, or dogma concerning the origin of man. Man is here. Man had an origin. These are facts. The truth of the origin of man cannot be changed by any opinion. If the theory of the Lithologic Cycle is fact, then the evidence will bear it out. It is not up to me to prove or disprove anything. It is my duty to describe facts, observations, and logic in such a way that others may use it as a working tool to gain greater insight into the real truth. It is my desire to present some of the possible implications of the Lithologic Cycle concerning existing explanations as to the origin of man. It is my observation that all popular explanations of the origin of man depend on the truth of the theory of the Lithologic Cycle. The recognition of the existence of the Lithologic Cycle neither proves nor disproves any existing theory as to the origin of man. It does however, lend credibility to all of them. By the same logic, each of the theories as to the origin of man lend credibility to the truth of the existence of the Lithologic Cycle.

If modern man has been in existence on this earth for at least one hundred thousand years that the theory of evolution predicts, there are some interesting questions that can only be answered satisfactory by the existence of the turnover phase of the Lithologic Cycle. Where are the records of the civilizations that must have developed in the first nine tenths of that time. Written recorded history has it's beginnings within the last ten percent of that time. Writing appears to begin with several different languages simultaneously. This is like the history of the development of language and civilization was destroyed on the order of ten thousand years ago. Evidence exists for advanced civilization before the writing of any written accounts in existence today. Are we expected to believe that nothing happened for ninety thousand years then, all of a sudden, evidence for man's existence appears simultaneously at multiple diverse places on the earth? Are we expected to believe that modern man could not write for ninety thousand years then learned to write everywhere suddenly in many different languages? Did the population of the earth grow almost none for ninety thousand years then suddenly start growing and in ten thousand years over populate the earth? Was man an endangered species for ninety thousand years, or was the record of his past civilization destroyed some ten thousand years ago? The hard cold facts are, after much archaeological searching, there is scant evidence for the existence of civilization older than about ten percent of the time that the theory of evolution predicts modern man to have existed.

When viewed objectively, the evidence overwhelmingly indicates a recent rapid turnover phase. Even the theory of evolution demands it. It is incomprehensible to believe that biologically modern man has existed on this earth for even one hundred thousand years as required by the theory of evolution without leaving a record of his existence. The archaeological record begins only a few thousand years ago with the relatively suddenly bloom of complex societies complete with several unrelated written languages . The facts of archaeologically recorded history indicate the sudden emergence of the complex societies of man onto the surface of the earth on the order of ten thousand years ago. The archaeological facts also indicate the growth of a very small population of man to the immense population we see today all within that same time span. The theory of evolution demands that biologically modern man has had enough time to have populated the earth many times. The process of development of complex cultures, societies, and technologies that we see today would have been repeated many times over in the past. Yet there is essentially no archaeological history of this existence, only a long time gap then a sparse archaeological record of a possible non-modern human society. A recent rapid turnover phase with only a few human survivors accounts for this loss of the archaeological record. The validity of the theory of evolution demands a recent rapid turnover phase of the Lithologic Cycle.

The process of development of complex cultures, societies, and technologies that we see today, developed at the rate our recorded history indicates, should have been repeated many times over in the past if man has been around as long as the vast eons of time required by the theory of evolution would lead us to believe.

Ancient Flood Accounts and the Lithologic Cycle

Ancient flood accounts have been discounted by the scientific community in general as myth or legend. It has been assumed that the basis of these accounts has been wild imagination. In the history of modern science there has never been credible explanation of the source for the extreme volumes of water necessary to cover the earth to the required depths. Furthermore, there has been no credible explanation as to where all that water went after the flood. Therefore, all ancient flood accounts have been dismissed as legend or myth.

All of a sudden, with the recognition of the Lithologic Cycle, the need for a change in volume of water on the earth is gone. There is sufficient water to cover the surface of the earth to an average depth of over two miles. The only reason the continents stick out above the water is the average height of the continents is over three miles above the average level of the sea floor. With the recognition of the Lithologic Cycle comes the mechanism for the periodic short term temporary rising of the ocean floor and sinking of the continents. This makes periodic massive world wide flooding not only a possibility, but a certainty.

With this turn of events, ancient writings previously considered to be myth, can now be reconsidered to be possible eye witness accounts of the phenomena that we know did in fact occur at some time in the past. Some of them may be distorted due to being verbally passed down from generation to generation before being recorded in writing. Others may have been written down with more accurate detail. All of them have details that indicate a knowledge of that which would be predicted by the theory of the Lithologic Cycle. Some of them indicate a partial or local rapid turnover phase with local flooding and local extinction. All of them collectively with their accounts of a great flood or sinking coastal cities recorded in ancient writings indicate an ancient knowledge of at least one rapid turnover phase with accompanying mass extinction.

TOUCHING ON PHILOSOPHY- THE BLENDER FISHBOWL

Living on Earth is kind of like the cartoon depicting stress where the fish is living in a fish bowl which is actually a blender. The fish is constantly in danger of someone pressing the "ON" button. So also, is the earth. The period of time we are now living in is the seemingly everlasting phase. The inhabitants of the earth are content to believe in a Uniformitarianism sort of way that this is the way it always has been and will always be. However, every few thousand years the surface of the Earth may behave as though someone pressed the blenders momentarily on button. Due to the instability of the cold solid ocean floor being more dense than the hot liquid beneath it, every few thousand years the ocean floor rapidly slides off into the liquid below and new hot rock takes the place of the old ocean floor. This is the runaway subduction phase of the Lithologic Cycle. The runway subduction phase carries eroded continental material that has been spread out on the ocean floor back to and under the continent. This lighter material is deposited under the existing continent. In the following rebound phase of the Lithologic Cycle the lighter continental material that was deposited below the continent buoys the continent up. This results in what was formerly recognized as the mountain building episode. The existence of this phenomena has been seen in the recent past as sea floor spreading or continental drift. Even before that it was seen by geologists as some unknown mechanism responsible for the "mountain building episodes" of the past.

APPENDIX A: THE LEGEND OF ATLANTIS

The legend of the sinking of Atlantis is recorded in the writings of Plato. Supposedly the account had previously been preserved by being handed down from an old man in his 90's to a young man of about 10 years of age. If there is any basis for the legend it could be an account of runaway subduction. You be the judge:

> "But afterwards there occurred violent earthquakes and floods; and in a single day and night of misfortune all your warlike men in a body sank into the earth, and the island of Atlantis in like manner disappeared in the depths of the sea. For which reason the sea in those parts is impassable and impenetrable, because there is a shoal of mud in the way; and this was caused by the subsidence of the island." From Timaeus, by Plato, Written 360 BC, Translated By Benjamin Jowett. http://the-tech.mit.edu/Classics/Plato/timaeus.body.html

If this is in fact an account of runaway subduction I would expect not to find the lost city of Atlantis because it is most likely not only under water, but also under rock as well.

APPENDIX B: THE BIBLICAL RECORDNoah's Flood

Another example is the flood of Noah as recorded in the book of Genesis. In the light of what we predict from the Lithologic Cycle Theory, there are certain details of the written account that now make sense. Most likely, the locality where Noah built his ship was far inland. He was not near any ocean. This accounts for two details of the account. First was the razzing he got from his neighbors. But more significance is buried in the details of the account. Noah's first realization of the beginning of the flood was the arrival of the animals fleeing the rising sea level, he did not mention the earthquake and tidal wave one would expect if the locality were near the ocean. The elevation must have been significantly above sea level because the torrential rains from the increased evaporation of the oceans reached Noah's area before the arrival of the rising sea.

Gen. 7:6 ¶ Now Noah was six hundred years old when the flood of water came upon the earth.

Gen. 7:7 Then Noah and his sons and his wife and his sons' wives with him entered the ark because of the water of the flood.

Gen. 7:8 Of clean animals and animals that are not clean and birds and everything that creeps on the ground,

Gen. 7:9 there went into the ark to Noah by twos, male and female, as God had commanded Noah.

Gen. 7:10 And it came about after the seven days, that the water of the flood came upon the earth.

Gen. 7:11 In the six hundredth year of Noah's life, in the second month, on the seventeenth day of the month, on the same day all the fountains of the great deep burst open, and the floodgates of the sky were opened.

Gen. 7:12 And the rain fell upon the earth for forty days and forty nights.

Gen. 7:17 Then the flood came upon the earth for forty days; and the water increased and lifted up the ark, so that it rose above the earth.
Gen. 7:18 And the water prevailed and increased greatly upon the earth; and the ark floated on the surface of the water.
Gen. 7:19 And the water prevailed more and more upon the earth, so that all the high mountains everywhere under the heavens were covered.
Gen. 7:24 And the water prevailed upon the earth one hundred and fifty days.
Gen. 8:1 But God remembered Noah and all the beasts and all the cattle that were with him in the ark; and God caused a wind to pass over the earth, and the water subsided.
Gen. 8:2 Also the fountains of the deep and the floodgates of the sky were closed, and the rain from the sky was restrained;
Gen. 8:3 and the water receded steadily from the earth, and at the end of one hundred and fifty days the water decreased.
Gen. 8:4 And in the seventh month, on the seventeenth day of the month, the ark rested upon the mountains of Ararat.
Gen. 8:5 And the water decreased steadily until the tenth month; in the tenth month, on the first day of the month, the tops of the mountains became visible.

Opening passages of The Bible

The ancient recorded history of the Bible opens with what appears to be a description of a rapid turnover phase of the Lithologic Cycle. This appears to be the original emergence of the continents from below sea level.

In the first two verses the subject is introduced describing the condition of the planet to be covered with water with no continents above sea level:

> *"In the beginning God created the heavens
> and the earth. And the land masses
> [earth/continents] had not formed, there were
> none, and darkness was over the surface of
> the ocean and the Wind of God was blowing*

*over the surface of the waters."...*Genesis 1:1,
2 translated from the original language.

The next six verses go back in time and describe a
few details of the various stages of development to
arrive at that point in time. The details include what
scientists recognize as what they call the" big bang"
where light is produced from nothingness, the
development of the atmosphere, and the filling of
the oceans by the atmosphere capturing water from
outer space.

At that point the narrative of the emergence of the
land masses continues:

> "*Then God said, "Let the waters below the
> heavens be gathered into one place, and let
> the dry land appear"; and it was so. And God
> called the dry land earth, [land
> masses/continents] and the gathering of the
> waters He called seas; and God saw that it
> was good."*...Gen. 1:9,10 (NASB)

The above opening verses of the bible appear to be edited
from a passage of scripture written earlier where more
detail is given:

> *4 Where wast thou when I laid the foundations of
> the landmass?
> declare, if thou hast understanding.*
> *5a Who hath laid the measures thereof, if thou
> knowest? or*
> *5b Who hath stretched the line upon it?*
> *6a Whereupon are the foundations of the foundations
> fastened? or*
> *6b Who cast out the corner stone thereof;*

*7a When the first generation stars were blowing out
        together,*
7b And all the members of God gave a blast?

8a Or [who] shut up the sea with doors,
8b When it [the landmass] brake forth,
8c [as if] it had issued out of the womb?
9a When I made the cloud the garment thereof,
9b And thick darkness a swaddlingband for it,
10a And brake up for it my decreed [place],
10b And set bars and doors,
*11a And said, Hitherto shalt thou [the sea]
        come, but no further: and*
11b Here shall thy proud waves be stayed?
            Job 38:4-11 (Translated from the original
                                            language)

This description of the emergence of the continents is
strikingly accurate to what would be predicted by the
Lithologic Cycle Theory.

The archaic language of some English translations could
well be clarified: The "surface of the deep" is the surface
of the oceans. The "deep" covering the continents is
water. The "surface of the waters" was the outer surface
of the planet earth because the continental land masses
were covered with water.

The darkness may possibly be a description of a cosmic
night caused by a catastrophic event documented to have
caused the triggering of some mass extinction events—
such as the meteorite strike at the end of the age of the
dinosaurs.

Incidentally, the mass extinction at the end of the age of
the dinosaurs probably included the mechanism of the

turnover phase predicted by the Lithologic Cycle Theory. During that catastrophic event it has been documented that the planet earth experienced deformation even to the opposite side of the planet. If an extraterrestrial impact would trigger a turnover phase of the Lithologic Cycle Theory, this event is an obvious candidate.

The next few verses of the Bible go on to describe the rebound phase predicted by the theory of the Lithologic Cycle, including the details of the continents emerging above the water and the development of life and ecology.

Over four hundred years later, still over three thousand years ago, when he laid out the chronology of the origin events, King David wrote:

> *5[Who] laid the foundations of the land masses,*
>   *(liquid mantle)*
>   *[that] it (land masses) should not be removed*
>   *for ever.*
> *6Thou coveredst it (mantle) with the ocean as*
>   *[with] a garment:*
>   *the waters stood above the mountains.*
> *7At thy rebuke they fled;*
>   *at the voice of thy thunder they hasted away.*
> *8The mountains go up, the valleys go down*
>   *unto the place which thou hast founded for*
>   *them (where they are in equilibrium).*
>   Psalms 104:5-8(Translated from the original
>   language)

Putting the dogmatism of the interpretation by theologians aside, ignoring the unresolvable differences in the dogma of interpretation or time scales, the original language of the Bible has no arguments with the Lithologic theory and has very accurate descriptions of what is predicted by the Lithologic theory.

Other Bible references to Lithologic Cycle events

Another interesting passage is what appears to be the description of a repeating, mass extinction cycle which is strikingly parallel to the predictions of the Lithologic theory. Notice the first part is in the past tense and uses the exact same original language expression as in the first verses of the bible describing the condition of the planet earth before the emergence of the continents. Also notice the last part is in the future tense, describing yet another repetition of something similar to the flood of Noah. Notice also in both cases there is a phase where there is darkness, or no light, similar to the Genesis and Job descriptions.

Jer. 4:23 I looked on the earth, and behold, {it was} formless and void; And to the heavens, and they had no light.
Jer. 4:24 I looked on the mountains, and behold, they were quaking, And all the hills moved to and fro.
Jer. 4:25 I looked, and behold, there was no man, And all the birds of the heavens had fled.
Jer. 4:26 I looked, and behold, the fruitful land was a wilderness, And all its cities were pulled down Before the LORD, before His fierce anger.
Jer. 4:27 For thus says the LORD, "The whole land shall be a desolation, Yet I will not execute a complete destruction..
Jer. 4:28 "For this the earth shall mourn, And the heavens above be dark, Because I have spoken, I have purposed, And I will not change My mind, nor will I turn from it."
Jer. 4:29 At the sound of the horseman and bowman every city flees; They go into the thickets and climb among the rocks; Every city is forsaken, And no man dwells in them." (NASB)

Other places in the Bible mention is made of Lithologic Cycle events in the context of daily living or future predictions:

Prov. 8:25 "Before the mountains were settled, Before the hills I was brought forth;

Is. 54:9 "For this is like the days of Noah to Me; When I swore that the waters of Noah Should not flood the earth again, So I have sworn that I will not be angry with you, Nor will I rebuke you. Is. 54:10 "For the mountains may be removed and the hills may shake, But My lovingkindness will not be removed from you, And My covenant of peace will not be shaken," Says the Lord who has compassion on you.

Mic. 1:4 The mountains will melt under Him, And the valleys will be split, Like wax before the fire, Like water poured down a steep place.

Matt. 24:35 "Heaven and earth will pass away, but My words shall not pass away.
Matt. 24:36 "But of that day and hour no one knows, not even the angels of heaven, nor the Son, but the Father alone.
Matt. 24:37 "For the coming of the Son of Man will be just like the days of Noah.
Matt. 24:38 "For as in those days which were before the flood they were eating and drinking, they were marrying and giving in marriage, until the day that Noah entered the ark,
Matt. 24:39 and they did not understand until the flood came and took them all away; so shall the coming of the Son of Man be.

Luke 17:26 "And just as it happened in the days of Noah, so it shall be also in the days of the Son of Man:
Luke 17:27 they were eating, they were drinking, they were marrying, they were being given in marriage, until the day that Noah entered the ark, and the flood came and destroyed them all.

2 Pet. 3:4 and saying, "Where is the promise of His coming? For {ever} since the fathers fell asleep, all continues just as it was from the beginning of creation."

2 Pet. 3:5 For when they maintain this, it escapes their notice that by the word of God {the} heavens existed long ago and {the} earth was formed out of water and by water,

2 Pet. 3:6 through which the world at that time was destroyed, being flooded with water.

2 Pet. 3:7 But the present heavens and earth by His word are being reserved for fire, kept for the day of judgment and destruction of ungodly men.

2 Pet. 3:8 But do not let this one {fact} escape your notice, beloved, that with the Lord one day is as a thousand years, and a thousand years as one day.

2 Pet. 3:9 The Lord is not slow about His promise, as some count slowness, but is patient toward you, not wishing for any to perish but for all to come to repentance.

2 Pet. 3:10 But the day of the Lord will come like a thief, in which the heavens will pass away with a roar and the elements will be destroyed with intense heat, and the earth and its works will be burned up.

2 Pet. 3:11 Since all these things are to be destroyed in this way, what sort of people ought you to be in holy conduct and godliness,

2 Pet. 3:12 looking for and hastening the coming of the day of God, on account of which the heavens will be destroyed by burning, and the elements will melt with intense heat!

2 Pet. 3:13 But according to His promise we are looking for new heavens and a new earth, in which righteousness dwells.

Rev. 21:1 And I saw a new heaven and a new earth; for the first heaven and the first earth passed away, and there is no longer {any} sea. (NASB)

APPENDIX C: THE PHILOSOPHY OF SCIENCE

One would like to believe that true science is looked up to and respected for being the unbiased discoverer, arbitrator and disseminator of truth. That fact puts science in the field of philosophy. Science is more than a collection of facts that are true. Science has become a set of beliefs by which one lives that are derived by direct observation of the evidence without the bias of some authority. At least, the one who believes he is living by a set of scientific beliefs believes that they are derived by direct observation of the evidence without the bias of some authority. However, Confirmatory bias is a fundamental feature of human nature.

Confirmatory bias is the tendency for human beings to more readily accept evidence that agrees with what they already believe and to more readily reject evidence that disagrees with what they already believe. It is a constant emotional fight to avoid succumbing to confirmatory bias. Are scientists exempt? No. Confirmatory bias is the bane of religion and science alike. In this respect, there is very little difference between science and religion.

Science does not know all the answers. That is what makes science such an exciting field of study. There are many truth's left to be discovered. As long as science limits it authority to realms where the answers can be known, and limits its pronouncements to that what is known to be fact, not theory, science can live up to that respected status. However, scientists are human, and as such are not very humble when they think they know more than non-scientists. Scientists sometime speak with false authority when they depend upon theories or hypothesis which are beyond the realm of the validated truth. It is then that scientists must be careful of confirmatory bias. When science depends upon a philosophical viewpoint to filter the evidence, it is guilty of confirmatory bias. When science is guilty of confirmatory bias, it can no longer be seen as an objective judge of the validity of truth. Too often has this been the case. History is full of examples. We are critical of the times when people believed that the earth was flat, frogs came from mud and flies came from meat. To us now the truth in these areas is obvious. Yet, we have been faced with the obvious in many other areas and have not recognized it. In a way, we, as scientists, have not advanced far in our way of thinking from the times we criticize.

Has science in the past lived up to that elevated status? Does science in the present live up to that lofty ideal? Will science in the future be able to retain that elevated position in the eyes of the general population? You be the judge. And then live your life by your judgments. But you must call it your philosophy, not science.

THREE PHILOSOPHIES OF GEOMORPHOLOGY

The science of geomorphology recognizes the fact that the topography of the continents that we find today is the combined result of the geology of the underlying rocks and the external elements of erosion. Rocks of differing hardness, shape, and orientation strongly influence the differing topographic features of the landscape. Current philosophies of geomorphology do not recognize the effect of some of the implications of the lithologic cycle. To the current philosophies of geomorphology, such things as the mechanism behind mountain building episodes are still in the realm of mystery.

Basically there are three differing philosophies or theories of the pre-historic development of the topography of the earth, life on the earth, man, and civilization. The point in time where archaeology takes over from recorded history is very soft. Recorded history is less universally accepted as the time span back from the present increases. What some hold to be recorded history, others, whose philosophy disagree with the teachings of the recorded history, believe it to be more legend or myth than factual. However, all agree that the written records of the past that we now have were written no earlier than about ten thousand years ago. Archaeological records earlier in time than the first recorded history are very scant. The absence of abundant archaeological records predating the development of written language by many thousands of years gives rise to many questions of our explanations of the origin of man as currently accepted by our scientific communities.

THE PHILOSOPHY OF CATASTROPHISM

The first philosophy accepted by the early scientific community was the philosophy of catastrophism. That which exists today did not get here via the forces we see working today at the rates we see them currently working. Certain catastrophic events in the past gave rise to what we see in the present. That philosophy was religious in nature and was based on the Bible being the Divine authority, and the traditional interpretation of the bible as influenced by the antique science of the Greek culture through which the bible has been handed down. Being religious in nature, certain interpretations by secondary authorities of what the original authority said became the dogmatic tenants of the philosophy and impeded true research of actual observations by scientists.

THE PHILOSOPHY OF UNIFORMITARIANISM

The second philosophy was popularized by James Hutton in the late 1700's when he published his *Theory of the Earth*. This philosophy claims to be scientific in nature. It originally was applied to geomorphology. (Later, Darwin based his theory of evolution on this philosophy when he published his book *The Origin of the Species*.) It is the philosophy of Uniformitarianism. That philosophy states that all that exists today come to be by the application of the processes we see working in the environment today at the rates we see them working today. For example, the Grand Canyon has a stream running in the bottom. For a stream that size to carve the Grand Canyon from rocks as hard as we see them today would take hundreds of thousands of years. Uniformitarianism philosophy says that is exactly how the Grand Canyon got there.

THE PHILOSOPHY OF MYSTERY The third philosophy is a philosophy of mystery. It is a philosophy that accepts the fact that we do not know everything. Mysterious occurrences in the past are responsible for what is in existence today. It is a strange mixture of science and religion and sometimes borders on science fiction. The philosophy of mystery has roots in the distant past. This philosophy is also well entrenched today among those who rebel against the arrogant dogmatism of the currently reigning philosophy.

THE RELIGIOUS NATURE OF SCIENTIFIC PHILOSOPHY

The basic problem is the idea that a scientist can speak with authority, yet a religious leader cannot speak with authority. That is a contradiction of philosophies. A scientist need not speak with authority, because the truths spoken, if they are true, stand without the authority. A fact is not true or false depending on who says it, it is true or false by it's own virtue. Just because a scientist speaks many truths, does not make him an authority that can change a statement into truth when what he speaks is not true. This also follows with religious leaders. Speaking a truth or untruth does not make it true or untrue in any realm. Truth is true, and fallacy is false. However, a religious leader can speak with authority in an area of unproven truth, because unproven truth is the realm of authority. A way of living can be just as viable when dictated by an authority whether it is based on fact or just on the authority of the leader. That is the difference between science and religion.

Religion is a set of beliefs by which one lives that are based on the teachings of some authority. Science is a set of beliefs by which one lives that are derived by direct observation of the evidence without the bias of some authority. For example it is scientific, not religious, to turn on a light switch or go to sleep at night because you know from personal experience that the light will go on or you will have another day tomorrow. It is religious, not scientific, to take some medical treatments on the order of a doctor when you do not know from personal experience that it will help. You only know that someone else has faith in the doctor or that sometimes what the doctor has prescribed did help, proving the doctor is an authority. (It is because of this religious faith in science that many medical procedures continue to be performed and paid for despite the fact that clinical tests prove no efficacy.) All of us have belief systems by which we live that are part scientific and part religious. It is when scientists speak with authority outside the realm of the true verifiable facts that they then become religious in their teachings.

Historically, in the development of modern science, the philosophy of catastrophism was the first philosophy to be accepted by the scientific community. Scientists of that day were convinced that the age of the earth was less than ten thousand years. This is because of the acceptance of the authority of the leaders of the religious community. There were so many things for which they had no other explanation if the age of the earth was less than ten thousand years. With the introduction of the philosophy of Uniformitarianism there was a release from the constraints of the authority of the religious community. For many, this has been praised as the greatest event in the development of scientific thought. They believed that it had freed the scientific world from the dogmatism of religion.

However as the philosophy of Uniformitarianism became entrenched in the scientific community it became like a religion. Their new found freedom from religion was just as binding as the old religion. The language of science adopted many words whose definition assumed the fact of the theories of Uniformitarianism. Scientists had to learn and use this language to be accepted among the scientific community. The required use of this philosophically tainted language prevented heretical expression of opposing or even questioning points of view from being published in any of the accepted scientific journals. This has been a demonstration of just how dogmatic scientists can be as they have held to the strict interpretations of their philosophy. Essentially all approved scientific interpretation of evidence is done with a bias toward the commonly accepted theory of evolution. The scientific world is again held captive to the dogmatism of religion.

This gave rise to renewed interest in catastrophism in the form of the Creation Science movement. There are just too many things that don't fit the strict Uniformitarianism interpretation.

And then there is the group of people that see the dogmatism of both sides and take it for a cover up. They see things that are not satisfactorily explained by either group and come up with an explanation of their own. These are the people who hold to the tenants of the third philosophy, the philosophy of mystery.

In a way, all of the philosophies are religious in nature in that their adherents are all dogmatic in that any explanation of the evidence must be in agreement with their authority, and any authority is outside the strict guidelines of Science.

POLITICAL CORRECTNESS AND SCIENTIFIC PHILOSOPHY

The greatest hindrance to the acceptance by the scientific community of the theory of the Lithologic Cycle may be that it is not politically correct. Specifically, the implication of a recent rapid turnover phase with it's resetting of man's technological and cultural development is not politically correct. It is not politically correct in that it lends credibility to the historical accounts of a world wide flood that have been documented in nearly all cultures and especially the account in the recorded history of the Bible. The fact is that the acceptance of the idea of a recent rapid turnover phase neither proves nor disproves the existence of God. The reluctance of the scientific community to accept the idea of a recent rapid turnover phase merely illustrates the politically correctness of extreme reluctance to accept the evidence of recorded history when that recorded history is in a religious context.

PHILOSOPHY WITHOUT RELIGION OR POLITICS

All these predominant philosophies are impeding true science. It is time for an era of objective evaluation of scientific evidence. This lack of objectivity is obvious for everyone to see It is time for someone to stand up and tell the world that "The Emperor Has No Clothes." True science needs to become unimpeded by the religious adherence to theories that are used as philosophies rather than tools. True science uses hypothesis and theories to help discover more truth by predicting and then testing the predictions. A hypothesis or theory should be used as a tool, not as a rule. It is false science that uses a theory as an authority to stifle and impede the discovery of truth.

The world needs to take a fresh look at the evidence unimpeded by the politically popular interpretation of the commonly accepted philosophies or theories. For example, infrequently occurring events such as the mountain building episodes mentioned earlier, being never directly observed (by currently accepted credible witnesses) would not be readily accepted to be within the philosophy of Uniformitarianism. However, all the forces and mechanisms that result in those infrequent episodes are observed in other combinations, and therefore would fit into the philosophy of Uniformitarianism if the scientist had an open mind.

Certain catastrophic events can now be accepted to conform to the philosophy of Uniformitarianism. The observation of actual events such as the rapid petrification of fossils due to the Mt. Saint Helens eruption, and the observation of actual physical evidence of past convulsions of the earth's surface such as the recently sunken slab of Pacific ocean floor standing vertically under the western side of the Americas has expanded the phenomena accepted to be part of the definition of Uniformitarianism.

Reinterpretation of the hypothetical mechanism for many of the geomorphic structures observed in nature is now in order. For example, entrenched meanders have long been considered to be the result of millions of years of simultaneous uplift and erosion of hard rock. Now an alternative hypothesis of rapid uplift and rapid erosion of soft, recently deposited sedimentation after a recent rapid turnover episode can be objectively considered.

We all live by what we believe. My definition of believe is not the mere acceptance of some idea, but the profound driving force that causes us to take the actions that we do. We take the action of turning on the light switch because we believe that will cause there to be light. The details and mechanisms are insignificant. When we want light we turn on a switch.

We all have a belief system based partly on science and partly on religion. Scientific belief is confidence in fact derived from first hand knowledge of fact such as hot burns and free objects fall. Religious belief is confidence in fact derived from the belief of some authority. We religiously believe most things because someone told us so. Some of us experiment more and thereby have a more

scientifically based belief system. No one has a purely
scientific belief system because we are constantly
bombarded by language.